Greek
Pottery Painting

Greek
Pottery Painting

Paolino Mingazzini

Paul Hamlyn

LONDON · NEW YORK · SYDNEY · TORONTO

Translated by F. B. Sear from the Italian original
Ceramica Greca
© *1966 Fratelli Fabbri Editori, Milan*
This edition © *1969*
THE HAMLYN PUBLISHING GROUP LIMITED
LONDON · NEW YORK · SYDNEY · TORONTO
Hamlyn House, Feltham, Middlesex, England
Text filmset in Great Britain by
Yendall & Co. Ltd., London
Printed in Italy by
Fratelli Fabbri Editori, Milan

GREEK POTTERY PAINTING

Of all forms of Classical art, Greek pottery affords the most complete and immediate pleasure to anyone who studies it. Most Greek vases are as beautiful today as when they left the hands of their makers. This does not mean that every vessel is beautiful in all respects; but even when its painted decoration is mediocre, its profile is generally speaking a perfect work of art in its own right. Whatever the shapes or proportions, the result is always one of supreme harmony.

In addition to the aesthetic pleasure to be derived from a thing of beauty, Greek pottery has great power to evoke the past. It records the spiritual, intellectual and everyday life of a civilisation, complementing the written sources. And, besides, it provides evidence for the reconstruction of the development of Greek painting. The record is, of course, incomplete and one-sided; but we possess only crumbs of knowledge, and each crumb is precious.

In descriptions of Greek pottery, it was until quite recently common practice to exclude everything that dated before 1000 BC because it was thought that the Greeks had not appeared in Greece before then. However, it is now known that they had arrived by at least the second half of the 2nd millennium BC. For the last few years we have been in a position to read certain documents used for accounting which date from before 1200 BC. They are written in a curious, rudimentary script, but the language is indisputably Greek. Plate 1 shows a fine example of the pottery of this period, which is normally referred to as 'Mycenean'. It is a long-stemmed goblet. The exquisite elegance of the profile contrasts with the highly stylised design of an octopus, which is nonetheless an effective piece of decoration.

Amid the general decline of Mycenean civilisation artistic skills in fact survived, but their freshness and naturalism faded along with the Creto-Mycenean world. The limits imposed upon this work forbid detailed treatment of the period; the shapes of the vessels and the decorative schemes are so numerous and varied that it would require ten times as many illustrations to give an adequate impression of the Mycenean achievement. It is necessary to pass over the centuries during which the Dorians destroyed the beautiful but fragile Mycenean civilisation, and to look at an *amphora* (plate 2) which comes from a group of tombs at Athens. It was made at a time when the city was just an agglomeration of small villages—though it was nonetheless the only centre of art and civilisation in the whole of mainland Greece. (What was happening in the Greek parts of Asia Minor is unknown.) Outside Athens, the 12th-8th centuries BC were a Dark Age of which nothing is known but the little the Attic tombs tell us.

Athens was the exception because it lay outside the main course of the invasions (probably because of its poor soil), and was thus spared from the destruction and pillage of war. (But though comfort and security are necessary conditions for civilisation, they are not its causes; and they certainly do not account for the rise and development of a civilisation such as that of Athens.)

Greek art is in large measure the product of two conflicting and interacting tendencies: the urge to represent life as it is, and an ideal of beauty that aims at perfection of form. The two are ineradicable elements of the Greek spirit, and war with each other in every object, however humble or elevated. The result was that neither beauty nor realism ever ousted the other; they were in tension—or, in the supreme achievements—wonderfully fused.

The large *amphora* reproduced in plate 2 was originally placed on the top of a funeral mound. In a society too poor for marble monuments it served as a marker for those who went to fulfil the ritual funerary rites. Apart from a band round the bottom (where the *amphora* was inserted into a base on the top of the funerary mound), the whole surface is covered with bands of geometrical ornament like lines of embroidery. There are figures on only two bands: one, around the neck, of grazing fawns; and the other, between the two handles, of a group of mourners standing around a funeral bier. Even these are just a combination of circles and triangles with very few concessions to reality—as if the artist were very reluctantly entering the real world. But he was

1. Goblet. Late Mycenean. 13th century BC. British Museum, London.

1.   Goblet. Late Mycenean. 13th century BC. British Museum, London. This goblet is decorated with an octopus so stylised that it would be difficult to recognise it as such, were it not that numerous other representations of the same subject exist. It was at first rendered realistically, but became increasingly stylised over a period of three centuries, ending as a purely geometric curved line.

2.   *Amphora.* Late Geometric. About the mid-8th century BC. National Archaeological Museum, Athens. Some areas are decorated with stylised human and animal figures. The *amphora* comes from the necropolis near the Dipylon gate at Athens. ('Dipylon' means 'double gate'; it did not exist in the 8th century.)

3.   *Amphora.* Protoattic, *c.* 700-670 BC. Louvre, Paris. This vase comes from Attica. Notice that the horses (a traditional subject) are more correct anatomically than the sphinxes (a new subject). The number and variety of filling ornaments in the background exemplifies the reluctance of artists—extremely marked at this period—to leave any space empty.

2. *Amphora.* Late Geometric, *c.* mid-8th century BC.
National Archaeological Museum, Athens.

entering it, all the same. In fact, the artist wanted to portray the world realistically, but was technically incapable of it. The achievement of technical mastery was to be a process of centuries.

The subject in the band between the handles was probably specified by the buyer. He was certainly a man of some importance, if only in a small village, who wanted to immortalise the last rites around the funeral bier. The drawing is quite 'childish', and it is difficult for 20th-century people to appreciate the mentality which created it. To avoid confusion the artist has painted the corpse separate from the bier on which it lies, so that it seems to hang suspended above it. The canopy which protected the body from the rays of the sun is shown hanging vertically, like a curtain, and the edges are trimmed to avoid obscuring the body. The horses have necks like giraffes and snouts like the closed flowers of poppies. The chest of the dead man is a black triangle; his head is like a round plate, and is also black except for a small dot which the artist intended to be understood as the eye. The women, who had to strike their heads as a sign of mourning, are differentiated from the men by a dash intended to indicate their

3.   *Amphora.* Protoattic, *c.* 700-670 BC. Louvre, Paris.

breasts. The warriors can be recognised by the swords hanging at their sides.

The *amphora* demonstrates movingly the artistic vitality of the executant. For one thing is certain: the person who painted this bowl had seen nothing on which he could model his work. These painters did not learn their technique from a master; they started from scratch, untrained, and accumulated experience and knowledge in the course of the work they carried out. The positive side of the lack of tradition and transmission of skills was a great and unhindered capacity for experimentation. Greek artists regarded the knowledge they already possessed as secondary; they were interested in new and untried techniques. In less than two centuries (the Dipylon vase was made in about 750 BC) the Greeks had advanced further than the Egyptians had done in 2,000 years—for Egyptian art, although impressive and refined, was highly stylised and hardly developed at all.

Greek art progressed rapidly in the depiction of external reality. A comparison between plates 2 and 3 will establish the point. Plate 3 is an *amphora* with a dance scene, men and women being shown alternately, holding hands and clutching branches. The women are no longer nude as in the abstract figures of the Geometric period, and the long hair flowing over their shoulders differentiates them from the men. The scene shown in plate 4, some 80 years later, is still more advanced: an attempt to narrate visually the stories of Homer and Hesiod. A large portion of the vase is taken up with the flight of the Gorgon. The outlining is a little too harsh, but the group around the neck, of Hercules killing the centaur Nessos, is more fluid and natural.

A generation later, work of a completely different character appeared. During the second half of the 7th century the development of craftsmanship in metal—of relief work, of inlaying using either a precious ductile metal like gold or silver, or copper inlaid in bronze—occurred; it was to have considerable influence on pottery. Several vases of bronze have survived, and testify to the development of the arts of chasing and embossing. The long and minute descriptions of the shield of Achilles in the *Iliad* and of the shield in *The Shield of Hercules* (attributed to Hesiod), are evidently inspired by a type adorned with a variety of concentric zones, each a few inches

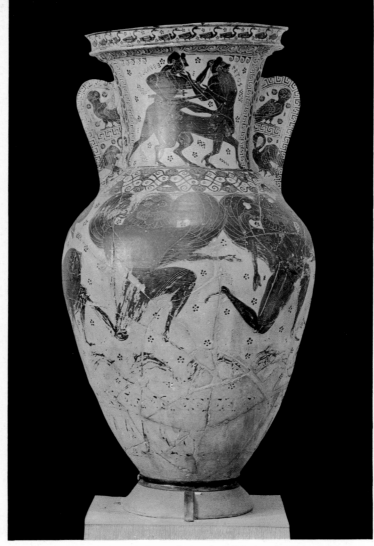

4. *Amphora.* Late Protoattic, end of 7th-beginning of 6th century BC. National Archaeological Museum, Athens.

5. Fragment of a *dinos*. First quarter of the 6th century BC.
National Archaeological Museum, Athens.

4.   *Amphora*. Late Protoattic. End of the 7th-beginning of the 6th century BC. National Archaeological Museum, Athens. It is also called the 'Nettos *amphora*' because of the representation around the neck, of Hercules killing the centaur Nessos. ('Nettos' is the archaic form of 'Nessos'.) The use of filling ornament is more sparing than in the previous example.

5.   Fragment of a *dinos*. First quarter of the 6th century BC. National Archaeological Museum, Athens. A *dinos* is a cauldron-shaped vessel; this example was found at Pharsalus in Thessaly. The banks of steps were the prototype of the stadium. Between the horses and the spectators is the painter's signature.

6.   *Oenochoe*. 7th-6th centuries BC. Museo di Villa Giulia, Rome. Found near ancient Veii; it is also called the 'Chigi vase' after the family which owned it. The surface is divided into zones, some of which are decorated with scenes from real life. Some authorities date it to 640-630 BC.; others (including myself) to 580-570 BC. Artist unknown.

7.   Large *crater* or mixing bowl, *c.* 570 BC. Museo Archeologico, Florence. Found at Chiusi. It is also known as the 'François vase' after its finder. It is signed by Ergotimos as potter and Klitias as painter.

8.   Column *crater*. 570-560 BC. Museo Gregoriano Etrusco, Vatican City. The folds of the drapery are flat and two-dimensional; the alternation of the three canonical colours, white, red and black, is very effective thanks to the clarity of the outlining; but the composition of the wedding-scene is frigid and stiff.

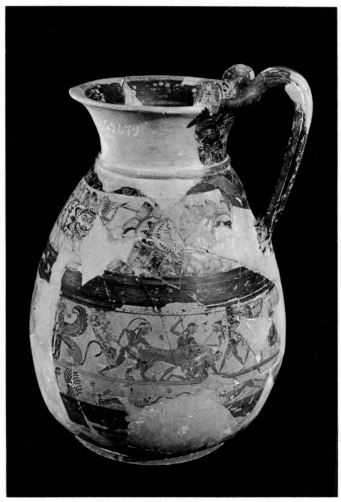

6.   *Oenochoe.* 7th-6th centuries BC. Museo di Villa Giulia,
Rome.

7.   Large *crater*, *c.* 570 BC. Museo Archeologico, Florence.

8. Column *crater*. 570-560 BC. Museo Gregoriano Etrusco,
Vatican City.

deep but at least four yards long, which could contain hundreds of figures and a great number of subjects. This kind of work appealed to one of the many facets of the Greek mind: love of perfection in miniature.

Elegance was much prized, and miniatures seemed to epitomise elegance. The works of the Corinthian vase painters of the 7th century, called in archaeological jargon 'Protocorinthian', were supremely elegant. Towards 570 BC, however, influenced by the narrative content of Attic pottery or inspired by metalwork, a number of works appeared which obviously derived from the relief technique flourishing in Corinth at the time. The finest example of this phase of Corinthian pottery is the Chigi vase (plate 6). The lion hunt painted on it displays both narrative ability and precision and grace in the rendering of minute details.

Such a development in Corinth could not fail to have repercussions in Athens, for the Athenian loved graceful miniatures as much as the Corinthian. The big *crater* usually known as the François Vase (plate 7) is packed with zones of small figures. Only two of these zones are purely decorative: one around the base, consisting of rays, and another with a pair of splendid griffins confronting each other over a fine palmette and lotus plant. On the same zone one can see a lion attacking a deer. It is realistically rendered, but is repeated four times to make a pattern.

This is certainly not true of the other five zones. Although the small scale of the figures makes it difficult to appreciate details, enough can be made out for one to be sure that in lively movement, complex grouping and variety of subject the François vase is in no way inferior to the Chigi vase. The first top zone shows the mythical Calydonian wild boar hunt, a subject well-suited to displaying the human figure in the various positions of combat. All the famous heroes of the past are assembled for this hunt, including a woman, Atalanta, recognisable by the white paint used to depict her flesh. (Not to mention the fact that her name, like those of the other figures, is written beside her!) On the second zone is a chariot-race. On the third, the most important because it is between the handles, gods in procession are bearing gifts on the occasion of the marriage of Peleus and Thetis. On the fourth Troilus is fleeing for his life from Achilles. Finally, around the foot is shown the fight between the pygmies and cranes.

This list, though incomplete (it does not include the other side, which was similarly decorated with mythical scenes), demonstrates that the painter, Klitias, was able to deal with scenes of every kind—epic, mythological, athletic and everyday. If relief work established a taste for small and precise figures, Klitias certainly knew how to exploit it, as is proved by the embroidered garments of the goddesses.

Side by side with the miniature style, Athens developed a style in which the paint brush played as big a part as the engraver's tool. This was the reason for her superiority over Corinth. For in the struggle between the engraving tool and the brush, the brush was ultimately to prevail. Plate 5 shows a sizeable fragment of a large vase signed by the painter Sophilos. It is a little earlier than the François vase. The figures are very small, but the incised details are not entirely accurate. Nor should one expect to find the painstaking accuracy—the attribute of a goldsmith rather than a painter—which is the hallmark of Klitias and the Chigi vase painter. This artist's preference was for the brush, which allowed him a greater freedom in details and produced more lively outlining.

And yet although the miniature technique died out in Corinth, it persisted at Athens—exclusively on cups, whose elegant profiles were suited to graceful decoration and series of minute figures.

The vase painters of Corinth rarely followed the lead of the great artists who were creating narrative scenes. Not that great artists were lacking in Corinth; but they limited themselves to repeating the same purely decorative animal scenes, whether real or fantastic. Even when a mixing bowl like that shown in plate 8, twenty years later than the François vase, has a subject taken from real life on its principal zone, its lower zone is decorated with a series of animals confronting but unrelated to each other. The goats graze and the panthers prowl, indifferent to the presence of attacker or victim. The upper zone does indeed contain a scene from real life: a husband driving his wife in a chariot in the presence of friends and relations. But their mannerisms are so stereotyped and their garments so monotonous! It is certainly a finished piece of work, with outlines that stand out sharply and neatly from the background, like the work of an engraver's tool—but nothing more.

9.   Large jug. Rhodian. 600-575 BC. Louvre, Paris. Called the 'Levy *oenochoe*' after its donor. Vases of this type are generally thought to have been produced on the island of Rhodes, but the attribution is not certain, for it is based solely upon the frequency with which vessels of this type turn up on the island.

10.   Corinthian jug. 580-570 BC. British Museum, London. This jug, from Camirus in Rhodes, is one of a type identifiable by the heraldic beasts facing each other, and by the rosettes in the background, which are blobs of paint scored with lines.

11.   *Amphora*. Corinthian. 560-550 BC. British Museum, London. Found on the island of Rhodes. Its decoration is in zones, with rosettes of different sizes between numerous somewhat schematically rendered animals. Some scholars date it to the last quarter of the 7th century.

9. Large jug. Rhodian. 600-575 BC. Louvre, Paris.

10. Corinthian jug. 580-570 BC. British Museum, London

11. *Amphora.* Corinthian. 560-550 BC. British Museum, London.

Outside Athens and Corinth narrative painting did not come into vogue so quickly, probably because the minor art centres did not have such an old tradition of painting. And, of course, pure decoration was much easier. However, during the first thirty years of the 6th century pottery makers whose works were of real value appeared in various centres in Greece. From this period comes the fine *oenochoe* shown in plate 9, the best and probably the earliest of the type, which is continually repeated in smaller versions with two instead of the five zones on this example. The goats and filling ornaments are practically identical, which suggests that they were done with a stencil. They are undoubtedly vases of great elegance; so fine that the slightest change would ruin their effect. They seem to have been produced in Rhodes, although this is not certain. The main decoration consists of an animal grazing, repeated along the same zone, as on the Dipylon vases 200 years earlier. But here they are extraordinarily accurate and lifelike, and incomparably more graceful.

In the middle years of the 6th century—say from 570 to 530 BC—there were many flourishing pottery centres throughout Greece, though none could approach the combined quantity, quality and variety of Attic products.

Corinth, as has been said, reluctantly followed the trend towards narrative painting. But, in compensation, so to speak, Corinthian craftsmen produced an enormous number of small vases, largely perfume flasks. Their quality inevitably declined as the quantity increased. The decline of Corinthian pottery was almost certainly a consequence of increasing demand for the contents of the vases; otherwise it would be difficult to explain why products so artistically inferior should have had such a vogue. Compare plate 10, for example—a jug of similar profile—with the Chigi vase. The old motif of the animal frieze persists, but with some innovations in doubtful taste, like the two panthers with one head between them and cocks' tails. The long, straight, drawn-out incision lines which mark off the limbs of the animals suggest that the artist was weary of his work.

Fortunately not all Corinthian pottery is like this. There is, for example, a delightful series of small perfume vases whose shapes are modelled on parts of the human body, animals or even pomegranates.

The most elegant appears in plate 12. It consists of four pomegranates joined together; a serpent, gripping a frog tightly in its mouth, is entwined around them. The original colours, black and a dark red, must have created an effect of sparkling gaiety. This might lead one to argue that there must have been a flourishing tradition of relief-work, anything but mediocre, in Corinth in the middle of the 6th century; if so, none of its products has come down to us. Works of quality are certainly rare in Corinthian pottery considering the quantity produced.

A pottery workshop flourished even in Sparta, but the workmanship was inferior and the subjects of little interest, with the sole exception of the cup in the Berlin Museum (plate 13). A line of warriors is returning from battle, carrying the dead body of a fallen comrade on their shoulders. They are all full citizens of Sparta, as can be seen from their long hair. This is a unique representation in art of that single-minded devotion to the state of which there is such an abundant record in written sources.

A completely opposite mentality is revealed by the water jug in plate 14, which comes from some part of Ionia; the exact site of the factory is unknown.

12. *Aryballos*. Corinthian. *c.* 550 BC. Museo Campano. Capua.

12. *Aryballos* or perfume flask. Corinthian, *c.* 550 BC. Museo Campano, Capua. In the shape of four pomegranates with a serpent devouring a frog twined round them. Unfortunately the colours have largely perished, but the sharply incised outlines provide a basis for reconstructing the original polychrome decoration. The pomegranates are decorated only at the bottom with two narrow bands of leaves and rosettes, but the scales of the serpent are painted individually.

13. Cup from Sparta. 530-525 BC. Staatliche Museen, Berlin. This cup, like all other examples from Sparta, exhibits the artist's inability to frame his subject in the space available. In later examples this problem is minimised by drawing a base line along the bottom and filling the space beneath it with small animals. This type of pottery is recognisable as Spartan because the figures are wearing long hair, which was the prerogative of first-class citizens.

14. *Hydria* or water pot. From Caere, 530-520 BC. Kunsthistorisches Museum, Vienna. Hercules is shown slaying King Busiris of Egypt and his priests. Like all the vases of this group —which have the same shape and differ from other contemporary vases by their gay, vivacious scenes—this example was found at Caere, modern Cerveteri. A fragment with an inscription has shown that this group comes from somewhere in Ionia in Asia Minor.

13. Cup from Sparta. 530-525 BC. Staatliche Museen, Berlin.

14. *Hydria* from Caere. 530-520 BC. Kunsthistorisches Museum, Vienna.

The scene is drawn from a myth which is otherwise little known. Hercules is a captive in the hands of King Busiris of Egypt, who sacrificed every stranger who wandered into his domains on the altar of his god. Without any resistance, Hercules allowed himself to be taken to the sacrificial altar; then he suddenly broke his bonds and slaughtered the priests. In this scene he has already strangled six, using his hands and feet; the rest are cowering, paralysed with fear. The least afraid is the king, recognisable by the *uraeus* (symbol of royal power) hanging around his forehead; he is writhing on the steps of the altar. The scene is utterly ludicrous, the tremendous power of Hercules making a ridiculous contrast with the pitiful weakness of the Egyptians. The comedy is increased by the figure of Hercules, more reminiscent of a gorilla than a Greek hero. Even at this early date, it seems, irreverence towards the gods was common in Ionia.

Sparta and Ionia, then, are opposites; between them stands Chalcis in Euboea. Vase painting is characterised by elegance tempered by a firm sense of restraint—that same stern elegance later found in Florentine art of the Quattrocento. Plate 17 is a good example. The Chalcidians shared the Attic predilection for narrative. This water jug shows Zeus hurling thunderbolts at Typhon, the winged monster whose body ended in two huge serpents' tails. It is an episode from the battle with the giants. There is an animal frieze too, but it is relegated to an unimportant place at the bottom. The products of other minor centres, for all their beauty and variety, are in no way comparable with the products of Athens.

The greatest artist of the generation following that in which the François vase was produced, was undoubtedly Exekias. His name is known because he signed several of his works. One of these is the *amphora* reproduced in plate 15. Exekias was demonstrably a pupil of Klitias, as can be seen from the miniature technique which he employs with such extreme fastidiousness: witness the cloaks and shields, not to mention the beards and hair, of the two warriors.

Technique aside, it was an amazing feat to achieve such a sense of the greatness of the participants in the scene; their heroic spirit is felt at once. The two great Athenian qualities—strength and grace—are held in perfect balance. In this work Exekias appears to cling to the miniature style of his master; in others, however, he emancipated himself from it completely without ever losing his precision in drawing. There is no trace of the miniature technique in the group of Achilles slaying Penthesilea (plate 16). The figure of the hero has an aura of grandeur; the queen, even though dressed as a warrior, is the embodiment of womanly grace. There is also an attempt to portray character: an attempt never made before. The expressions on the faces of the protagonists, confronting each other in the moment of death, raises the painting to the level of psychological drama. (The myth is described in the notes to plate 16.)

This vase was made in 530 BC, or a little later. At about this period one of the most important developments in the history of Greek pottery occurred: the beginnings of a new style with red figures on a black ground. In the space of thirty years it completely replaced the black-figure style. The reason for this innovation was the desire to express more effectively ideas which could not be fully expressed with the old technique. Incision produced lively surface treatment by means of a rigidly controlled colour scheme, and

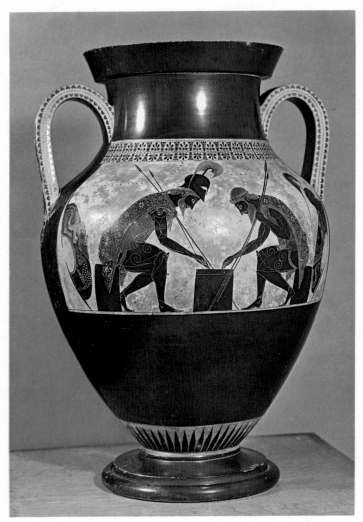

15. Large *amphora, c.* 530 BC. Museo Gregoriano Etrusco, Vatican City.

16. *Amphora.* 530-520 BC. British Museum, London.

15.   Large *amphora, c.* 530 BC. Museo Gregoriano Etrusco, Vatican City. From Vulci. It is signed by Exekias either as potter (that is, as designer of the shape and owner of the kiln) or as painter. The fact that he signed it shows that he was conscious of the quality of his work; a quality which is enhanced by sparing use of ornament. The episode of the two heroes, Ajax and Achilles, so absorbed in their game of draughts that they missed the crucial point in the battle (both are in full armour), probably appeared in a lost epic poem.

16.   *Amphora.* 530-520 BC. British Museum, London. From Vulci. This must also be mentioned in some lost epic. It is a duel between Achilles and Penthesilea, the Amazon queen, who declared her love for Achilles at the very moment when he slew her. The painter has given the queen a helmet, lance, sword and shield, but not a breastplate, perhaps feeling that a fine leopard skin would be more appropriate for a woman.

17.   Chalcidian *hydria,* 530-520 BC. Museum Antiker Klein-kunst, Munich. Photo Hirmer. Probably from Vulci. It shows Zeus struggling with the storm god, Typhon. All vases of this type are attributed to the city of Chalcis, in Euboea, on the basis of the dialect and alphabet used in the inscriptions.

17. Chalcidian *hydria.* 530-520 BC. Museum Antiker
Kleinkunst, Munich.

certain details, such as the folds of garments within the general shape of the figure, could be expressed. But it definitely did not allow scope for shading; and in fact the reversal of the colour scheme from black figures on a red ground to red figures on black was due solely to a desire for shading. In one of the very rare comments on the technique in ancient sources, it is expressly stated that Cimon of Cleonae—of whom nothing is known except that he was working at this period—discovered how to differentiate between shallow and deep folds on drapery and mark muscles and veins. It was clearly not possible to obtain this effect by scratching with a sharp point on an evenly coloured surface. The same source attributes another innovation to Cimon: the discovery of the formulae (called in Greek *mechanai* or 'tricks') of linear perspective. The ancient phrase is: 'how to draw figures at oblique angles and faces looking up, down and to the side'. With a caution and diffidence difficult for us to appreciate, used as we are to the most advanced techniques of the ancients, these innovations were incorporated into the repertoire of red-figure painters. It is fascinating to observe this process taking place step by step.

Two of the 'tricks' invented by Cimon were used just as much by black-figure as red-figure painters (more than one painter used both techniques on one vase). They are rudimentary, which is to say obvious —once discovered. One of them was to paint any circular object as an oval when seen from a three-quarter viewpoint. The other was to represent the fold on drapery by means of a zig-zag line. On the *amphora* in plate 16 both these techniques occur, although they have been adopted very cautiously and are only apparent on close scrutiny. Achilles' *chiton* ends with a zig-zag line at the bottom, which forms a series of steps. (The *chiton* was a flowing garment worn by women as well as men.) The folds that catch the light are red, those in shadow are black. The shields of Penthesilea and Achilles are not perfectly circular or in perfect profile, but exactly oval. All these innovations are found in the works of Exekias, though he never ventured into the realm of red-figure painting.

The black-figure style died only very slowly. The little figures of the miniaturists were particularly well suited to vases of small dimensions. Plate 18 shows a cup of very elegant proportions with an equally elegant strip of black-figure decoration concentrated in a narrow band on a line with the handles. Nine hunters are attacking the enormous Calydonian wild boar. The groups of hunters are rendered in a somewhat schematic manner reminiscent of Archaic work, but this does not detract from the vivacity of the scene. It is made all the more convincing by the presence of two dogs, one being torn to pieces by the boar, the other—a white dog— biting the boar's neck.

One of the first, possibly the very first painter to adopt the red-figure technique, was Oltos. One of his works, the huge cup from Tarquinia (plate 21), shows the Olympian gods seated at a solemn reception. The device of using zig-zags to represent folds is employed with greater sophistication: above all, they are less schematic than when they first appeared. The differentiation between shallow and heavy folds and thin and thick garments is also easier to perceive on this piece.

A vase in Berlin, not illustrated here, demonstrates that Oltos was unable to master some of the more difficult problems of perspective. But at any rate he tried to make use of the new means of expression, employing them with deep conviction while others were uncertain and reserved them for the less important parts of the vase. In plate 22, an unsigned cup which is, however, reliably attributed to Oltos, Priam is begging Achilles to return the body of his son Hector. The freedom and liveliness of the figures on this vase reveals the possibilities of the new technique. Its beauty is not, of course, a matter of technique alone: Oltos was the outstanding vase painter of his generation.

Not all clients, however, encouraged the new technique. For two decades it was applied almost exclusively to cups, and even so only on the outside. This was because cups were luxury goods, purchased only by the rich. Reference has already been made to a cup of the period 540-530 BC with the surface black-glazed except the narrow figured zone (plate 18). Plate 20 shows a cup made thirty years later on which the colour scheme has been reversed. The main body of the vase has been left the colour of the red ground, while the inside (plate 19) is completely glazed except for the medallion in the centre. On the medallion two goats face to face are making a trial of strength, standing on their hind legs and

18.   Cup. 540-530 BC. Museum Antiker Kleinkunst, Munich. This cup (from Vulci) is signed by two miniaturists, Archicles and Glaukytes. The scene is the Calydonian wild-boar hunt. The numerous inscriptions, indicative of the spread of Athenian culture at this early date, take the place of filling ornament.

19.   Attic cup. 510-500 BC. Castle Ashby, Northants. Collection of the Marquess of Northampton. This cup, signed by Tleson, is of unknown provenance, but it almost certainly comes from southern Etruria. Notable are the two goats confronting each other heraldically. The outlining is fluid and economical.

20.   Attic cup. 510-500 BC. Castle Ashby, Northants. Collection of the Marquess of Northampton. The graceful shape and very tall stem of the cup places it in the last decade of the 6th century BC. A red-figured cup from the workshop of Tleson has also survived. Sometimes he adds the name of his famous father, Nearchos, to his own.

21.   Cup. 510-500 BC. Museo Nazionale, Tarquinia. Found in a necropolis at Tarquinia; it is signed by Oltos as painter and Euxitheos as potter. This side shows a reception on Olympus; Zeus, with his cup-bearer Ganymede, Athena, Hermes, Hebe, Hestia, Aphrodite and Ares. On the other side is Dionysus and his retinue.

18. Cup. 540-530 BC. Museum Antiker Kleinkunst, Munich.

19. Attic cup. 510-500 BC. Castle Ashby, Northants.

20. Attic cup. 510-500 BC. Castle Ashby, Northants.

21. Cup. 510-500 BC. Museo Nazionale, Tarquinia.

butting each other. Every detail—the crown of black and purple leaves, the attitudes of the animals, the profile of the vase, the varicoloured fleeces of the goats and the palmette in the space underneath them—is extremely elegant.

The red-figure painters of the development period —the twenty years between 530 and 510 BC—will now be dealt with. The antithesis of Oltos was Epictetus, whose career began a little after the start of red-figure. Epictetus was of course acquainted with the black-figure technique; the medallion in plate 25, for example—a nobleman setting out for the hunt on horseback—is painted in black-figure on the inside of the cup. (The outside is painted on both sides in red-figure; an armed satyr between two huge eyes and two magnificent palmettes, preparing to fight.) The calm of the young horseman is in contrast to the ardour of the prancing horse, eager to gallop off. The sense of balance and harmony that enabled Greek artists to create effective compositions in such awkward picture shapes is quite astonishing.

The same elegance and skilful framing occurs in the tondo of another cup by Epictetus, this time in red-figure (plate 26). It shows an Amazon running, and at the same time taking an arrow from her quiver. The artist's signature can be seen at the edge of the tondo; he was obviously aware of the quality of his work. He has struck a harmonious balance between the figure and the empty spaces around it without distorting the proportions of the young girl. Her soldier's clothes do not conceal her femininity, but at the same time look perfectly natural. There is one technical point of interest: there is no zig-zag in the folds such as occurs on the previous figure. It suggests that painters of this period avoided displaying two innovations at once.

The works of minor artists demonstrate that differences of talent remained as important as technical matters. Plates 23 and 24 show two parts of a vase, the shoulder and the body, by one such minor artist, Phintias.

Plate 24 shows a music lesson. The music master is seated on the right; facing him, also seated, is his pupil. Another student stands between them, perhaps waiting his turn. Behind the student practising stands his father, watching his progress. The seated figures are correctly executed; artists often painted the human figure in this position. But the figure of the old man leaning on his stick is somewhat awkward because this posture had not been attempted before. His body is completely twisted, and his right arm is rather unsatisfactory. Evidently Phintias had not yet assimilated the new methods introduced by Cimon of Cleonae.

Plate 23 is a banquet scene: courtesans playing the game of *kottabos* (see plate notes). Here too Phintias has attempted a lively treatment; notice, for example, the way the women are spinning the vases around on one finger. The courtesan on the left is even raising her right leg to add more force to her throw. Nevertheless everything is rendered too stiffly, with nothing of the fluency of Epictetus.

The credit for having learnt to apply the innovations of Cimon correctly must go to Euphronios, a contemporary of Phintias. One of his signed works is a mixing bowl on which Hercules is shown struggling with Antaeus (plate 27). Even the elapse of twenty-four centuries does not prevent us from appreciating the feelings of Pliny (or his source) when he enumerated the merits of Cimon of Cleonae. The muscles of Antaeus are indicated with dark lines which indicate the areas of the body in shadow.

The giant's hair and beard are carefully differentiated from those of the hero; they are painted grey to show that the hair and beard of a Barbarian are thin and patchy, not thick and well-combed like those of a Greek. In spite of the struggle, not a hair is ruffled; the artist has even experimented with blobs of thick glaze at the ends of the hair. Extremely skilful too is Euphronios' rendering of muscles, in which he surpassed his contemporaries. But his greatest gift was in the complex arrangement of the two bodies locked in combat; such a group would have been unthinkable before Euphronios.

Euthymides was a worthy rival of Euphronios. Plate 30 shows a detail of an *amphora* painted by him. On it he unwittingly paid his rival the great compliment of taking his work as a standard of excellence, boasting that he had painted a picture 'such as Euphronios never did'. The subject is a young man about to finish putting on his armour in the presence of his parents. The light folds in the costume of the young warrior and his mother are outlined with dilute glaze; the heavy folds are in normal glaze. They represent a great advance on the simple zig-zag folds of Oltos, which are outlines without substance;

22. Cup. 510-500 BC. Museum Antiker Kleinkunst, Munich.

22.   Cup. 510-500 BC. Museum Antiker Kleinkunst, Munich. This comes from Vulci and is attributed to Oltos on stylistic grounds. Priam, king of the Trojans, is approaching Achilles to beg for the body of his son Hector; but Achilles signifies his refusal. Hermes withdraws, his mission complete.

23.   Detail of a *hydria*. 510-500 BC. Museum Antiker Klein- kunst, Munich. Two courtesans are playing a game of *kottabos*, which consists of throwing the dregs of a cup of wine at a balanced dish so as to make it fall over. This was normally played by men; whoever won had first choice of the women hired for the banquet. In this case, however, the positions are reversed.

24.   Detail of a *hydria*. 510-500 BC. Museum Antiker Klein- kunst, Munich. This detail of a *hydria,* which comes from Vulci, is signed by Phintias as painter. The subject is a music lesson. The works of Phintias exhibit a very refined technique and great attention to detail.

23. Detail of a *hydria*. 510-500 BC. Museum Antiker
Kleinkunst, Munich.

24. Detail of a *hydria*. 510-500 BC. Museum Antiker
Kleinkunst, Munich.

those of Euthymides are full, they have 'body' (Pliny calls it *'sinus'*, which means a bosom).

However, this analysis of the techniques involved should not obscure the interest of the subject-matter. A young warrior is lacing up his breastplate. His shoulderpieces are still undone. His mother is holding his helmet and lance while his father gives him some advice. The parents seem to be concerned only about equipping their son, but these practical activities do not conceal the sorrow of separation and anxiety about the son's future. The painting succeeds in expressing a mood as well as showing an action.

Many other works by the two rivals deserve to be mentioned, but the scope of this work permits only one more example, by Euthymides, (plate 29). This is a group of three drunks. Two of them are trying to prove that they are not really drunk by dancing on one leg—a sure sign that they *are* drunk. The third seems to be trying to defend himself from invisible enemies with a stick. More interesting than the subject itself are the formal problems it created; of course, the subject may have been decided upon in order to raise—and tackle—the problems. Among the innovations with which Pliny credits Cimon are the poses of the man 'looking behind, or up, or down', and the *'obliquae imagines'*, or foreshortening. Several of these features occur on this vase. The laws of perspective had not yet been fully grasped, of course: the man in the middle has turned his head through 180 degrees and is looking at his feet, which is not possible in nature. But the painter gets other things right: the right buttock of the same figure does not exactly cover the left, and his backbone is not perfectly vertical, but oblique. These things appear elementary now; but they were nonetheless a discovery without precedent, used with great caution by even the most gifted painters.

The twenty years preceding the Greek victory at Salamis saw the apogee of Attic painting (500-480 BC). In a book of this size only a few of the many important painters of the time can be discussed, and such a selection cannot be entirely representative. After being a painter dependent upon a potter, Euphronios himself became a potter. How or why this happened is not known, but he did select and teach painters, including two who produced surprisingly dissimilar works. One, whose name is unknown, is conventionally called 'the Panaitios painter'.

25. Inside of a cup. 520-510 BC. British Museum, London.

25. Inside of a cup. 520-510 BC. British Museum, London. It is signed by Epictetus as painter and Hischylos as potter. When two signatures occur on the same vase we of course know the artists are contemporaries; and this is invaluable in establishing chronology. The horseman is setting off for a hunt, not for war.

26. Inside of a cup. 520-510 BC. British Museum, London. It comes from Vulci, and is signed by Epictetus, whose name means 'one who is acquired' or 'slave'. Notice how perfectly the figure fits the tondo of the cup; head, arms and legs are all contained within the circle without the figure appearing distorted.

27. *Crater*. 510-500 BC. Louvre, Paris. Cliché des Musées Nationaux. This type of mixing bowl is cup-shaped, and is called a 'calyx *crater*'. It comes from Cerveteri and was painted by Euphronios. Hercules is shown struggling with Antaeus. According to the myth, Antaeus received fresh strength from contact with his mother, Earth; Hercules overcame him by lifting him bodily off the ground so that he lost the source of his strength. Notice the precision with which the muscles of the combatants are rendered.

26. Inside of a cup. 520-510 BC. British Museum, London.

27. *Crater.* 510-500 BC. Louvre, Paris.

The liveliness and precision of his drawing indicates that he was one of Euphronios' pupils. The subject in plate 28 is a rather difficult one, drawn with a light hand and treated with a touch of humour. The scene must be a banquet because of the hanging basket which would be full of bread. A courtesan has put aside her lyre: before demonstrating her musical ability she has been invited to perform a service of another kind. However, the knot of her garment is proving difficult to untie, and the client is somewhat peremptorily urging her to hurry up.

This belongs to a particular pictorial genre: the picture which captures the fleeting moment. From the technical point of view one must admire the unerring way the painter has set the two figures in the circle of the tondo. Each of them is given characteristics appropriate to the situation. The woman bows her head in token of obedience—and also to untie the rebellious knot; the man squats because he is waiting for her on the couch. The man's legs are treated surely, despite the fact that they are awkwardly drawn back under the couch. The looks on the faces of the characters are equally appropriate —the woman's submissive, the man's imperious.

The other artist who worked under Euphronios was called Onesimos. His ideal was grace and elegance (plate 31), and he sometimes came close to affectation. The Berlin painter had the same ideal of elegance and harmony, but pursued it in a completely different way. On the magnificent *amphora* from which the painter has been named, the group of Apollo, the deer and a satyr stand out in the centre of the vase. Nothing except a simple line which acts as the base and an ivy bough around the neck distracts the eye from the picture. Everything— proportions, poses, anatomical details and material objects—is polished, and precisely executed. Such work was an artistic climax—but one which could not be sustained without a decline into mannerism.

Fortunately Attic artists proved able to renounce the creation of isolated and perfect figures and pass on to more varied and complex scenes. The Cleo-phrades painter composed scenes of terrible violence and profound drama. In plate 32 Priam is seated on an altar with the body of Hector's young son, Astyanax, on his lap. Neoptolemus, heedless of the sacrilege he is about to commit, is dragging him off the altar in order to kill him more easily. At his feet lies a dead

Trojan; he has died gloriously, without abandoning his shield. On the right, a Greek is forced to defend himself against the desperate fury of Andromache, who attacks him with a table leg. On his left, a woman awaits her fate by the statue of Athena. Images of different kinds crowd before the eye of the spectator, the images of fate and war: the cruel slaughter of the defenceless, sacrilegious rape, a whole population in terror-stricken flight—the whole gamut of horrors is seen in rapid succession.

In the cup reproduced in plate 34 Douris dealt with the theme of Eos (Dawn) burying the body of her son. The contrast between the deathly stiffness of Memnon and the youthful grace of the goddess accentuates the tragedy already inherent in the premature death of a young man. The group has been compared with Michelangelo's *Pietà*—and not without reason, for in that too the youthful Madonna contrasts with Jesus, who is portrayed as a mature man.

Douris also liked to paint mythical scenes of dramatic rather than psychological content, for example Jason in his quest about to be gobbled down by the dragon who guarded the golden fleece;

Athena, protectress of the bold, obliges the monster to release its prey (plate 33). The size of the figures, extended to the very edge of the circle, reveals a certain uneasiness on the part of craftsmen like Douris, who were consciously or unconsciously tending to produce larger, more grandiose scenes in conformity with the wall paintings of the great contemporary artists.

With Brygos we enter a different world, one of banquets and easy women; the world glimpsed in the comedies of Menander—and one which certainly loomed large in the everyday life of the richer Athenians. Plate 35 shows a young man whose youthful inexperience has led him to drink too much, with the result that he is being sick. The very young courtesan is behaving like a sister rather than a lover. The subject could not be more prosaic or inelegant, but Brygos' skill is such that he manages to create beauty from an event that is itself ugly.

Wine, women and song were certainly close to the heart of Brygos, whose most happy works—perhaps the apogee of ancient vase painting—are precisely those which depict this world in all its aspects. In plate 36 a group of revellers, already

28. Inside of a cup. 500-490 BC. British Museum, London.

28.   Inside of a cup. 500-490 BC. British Museum, London. The cup comes from an Etruscan necropolis and bears the signature of Euphronios as potter. Because Panaitios was often praised as a perfect painter, the anonymous painter of this cup has acquired the name of 'the Panaitios painter'. The man's profile contains some realistic touches, for example the prominent nose and bald head, perhaps intended to indicate a vigorous and profligate character.

29.   *Amphora*. 510-500 BC. Museum Antiker Kleinkunst, Munich. It is signed by Euthymides as painter. He has chosen very complicated poses for his figures in order to experiment with new and difficult techniques. He has added to his signature, 'As Euphronios never did'—a taunt to his rival. The remark throws light on the rivalries that existed among painters of the period.

30.   Detail of an *amphora*. 510-500 BC. Museum Antiker Kleinkunst, Munich. This *amphora* comes from Vulci and is signed by Euthymides. The painter has depicted a scene from mythology and gives the figures the names of Hector, Priam and Hecuba; but the soldier looks more like a recruit than a legendary hero, and the figure of the mother corresponds exactly to the figures on Attic funerary reliefs of the 5th and 4th centuries.

29. *Amphora.* 510-500 BC. Museum Antiker Kleinkunst, Munich.

30. Detail of an *amphora*. 510-500 BC. Museum Antiker
Kleinkunst, Munich.

rather tipsy, is going off chattering to find a similar group. The three older men evidently feel the effects of the wine most. One is singing and throwing off his mantle because it is too hot; another is dancing a step or two; the third is waving his hands about, perhaps in a fit of jealousy. The three young men are in the service of the rich revellers, but bear themselves with dignity. One is playing a double flute, one the lyre and the third, overcome by the poignancy of the verses recited by the old man following him, is holding his head. The characters are well-defined psychologically; this, and the fluidity of line and harmony of shapes, make this a perfect scene.

This increasing interest in states of mind rather than action would have been impossible had not another advance in drawing technique taken place— one that seems small at first sight but was of incalculable importance. This was the discovery of how to depict the human eye in a three-quarter view, and later in full profile. The eye had always been painted frontally, with the pupil in the centre of an oval. But in the works of this period the pupils have been moved nearer to the nose, and that end of the oval has been left open. The eyes can now look in a specific direction and meet the eyes of another person.

Thirty years later another great vase painter, the Penthesilea painter, so called from the cup in plate 37, made the meeting of eyes the focal point of the picture. The subject is the well-known one of Achilles and Penthesilea, already discussed in relation to the black-figure *amphora* by Exekias. Here it is treated with much greater intensity. The expression in the heroine's eyes is more than a simple declaration of love: it speaks of complete, unbounded dedication. Two details, however, mar the beauty of the group: the presence of the two secondary figures (the Greek who is going away, not realising the drama unfolding right next to him, and the dead Amazon lying on the ground); and the overcrowded effect caused by the closeness of the border to the figures. Considering the size of the cup, this is surprising; it is one of the biggest cups extant, so big that it was clearly never envisaged as a functional object. The artist was evidently carried away by a wall painting he had seen, and tried to reproduce figures of like spirit and grandeur, cramming them into the tondo of a cup.

Many small masterpieces of the period could be

31. Cup. 480 BC. Musées Royaux d'Art et d'Histoire, Brussels.

31.   Cup. 480 BC. Musées Royaux d'Art et d'Histoire, Brussels. Onesimos' personality is displayed in this painting of the young girl with long hair preparing to take a bath; the whole scene is fitted into the tondo of the cup. The naturalness and elegance of the girl's pose is very striking.

32.   *Hydria.* 480 BC. Museo Nazionale Archeologico, Naples. This vase comes from Nola and its subject is the destruction of Troy. In the centre Ajax is dragging Cassandra away from the statue of Athena, where she has taken refuge, and Neoptolemus is killing King Priam. Although the scene is full of passion and movement, clarity and sharpness of outline is preserved.

33.   Inside of a cup. 480-470 BC. Museo Gregoriano Etrusco, Vatican City. This splendid cup, which comes from Cerveteri, is generally assigned to the last period of the painter Douris. The subject is taken from the myth of the Argonauts.

34.   Cup. 500-490 BC. Louvre, Paris. Cliché des Musées Nationaux. Comes from a necropolis in ancient Capua, and is signed by Douris as painter and Calliades as potter. The scene shows Eos, the goddess of dawn, carrying away her son Memnon after his death in a duel with Achilles. The drawing is steady and deliberate, in harmony with the emotion of the scene.

32. *Hydria.* 480 BC. Museo Nazionale Archeologico, Naples.

33. Inside of a cup. 480-470 BC. Museo Gregoriano Etrusco, Vatican City.

34. Cup. 500-490 BC. Louvre, Paris.

cited. For example, plate 38: Polynices offering the necklace of Harmonia to Eriphyle. (He hoped she would reveal the hiding-place of her husband, whose help in the war against Thebes Polynices wished to obtain.) This little drama is conveyed with hardly any movement on the part of the protagonists: the only gesture—Eriphyle's outstretched hand—epitomises the whole drama with great intensity. The same intensity is found in the Orpheus and Eurydice relief from Naples, and even before that, on the pediments of Olympia and also in the works of the first two tragedians. It was no coincidence that the first sophists appeared in these decades: it was they who taught the art of expressing essentials with the most exact words.

The great artists must be credited with the development in depicting the eye, because it is known that Polygnotus—the first Greek painter about whom more than the name is known—produced a great wall painting with Paris trying to attract the attention of Penthesilea. It was not, however, a very successful attempt.

This raises the difficult question of the relative standing of artist and craftsman. A difference between artist and craftsman undoubtedly existed in antiquity, although this has often been denied. This is the only explanation of the fact that ancient art historians record the names of the great artists, but do not mention—even to criticise—the wonderful vase painters or coin and gem engravers.

Naturally neither craftsmen nor buyers were in a position to keep up with an art which became increasingly elevated in tone and increasingly complex in its methods. For that reason, from 480 BC onwards there was an ever-widening breach between artists and craftsmen.

At this point let us examine two works produced by men of very different outlook, though separated by only a small gap in time. The first (plate 39) is a white-ground cup. On the tondo Aphrodite is being carried through the air on a swan; she is tightly wrapped up in her garments and only her right hand is visible, holding a flower.

By contrast Pauson broke with the whole tradition of the past, disregarding the Greek ideal of beauty; Aristotle used to say that Polygnotus improved on the human form, and Pauson detracted from it. From what can be deduced from chance references, his aims must have been diametrically opposed to those current at the time.

Nothing is known for certain of Pauson except that he painted a picture of a horse which appeared to be wallowing in the dust. A distant echo of his work perhaps appears in that of an unknown painter called 'the master of horses'. His horses (plate 42) are very different from the fine steeds of Epictetus and Euphronios. There are no elegant, sinuous outlines; the snout is decidedly ugly and the profile and the stance are unharmonious. But what tension, what vitality—and it is produced by the avoidance of harmony. Perhaps the horses that Pauson painted were like this. Perhaps the men he painted (which Aristotle said young men should not see in case their moral standards were lowered) inspired the painter of the battle with the Amazons, reproduced in plates 40 and 41. There is absolutely no beauty, harmony and nobility in these Amazons and Greeks. The Geneva painter—so called because this vase is in a museum there—is isolated, as Pauson was isolated.

The noble simplicity and restrained grandeur of the sculptures produced between 480 and 430 BC were extolled by Wincklemann and so delighted cultivated society during the reign of Hadrian that it became fashionable to have copies of them made. (This, incidentally, has been of great value to the historian.) The masterpieces of Olympia and the Parthenon were matched—if 5th- and 4th-century critics are to be believed—by great paintings in the same style. Yet in vase painting almost all the works inspired by the style combine extreme correctness of drawing with extreme stiffness. Very few of the works which strive for an effect of nobility or grandeur are in fact anything but empty and formal.

One of the exceptions (plate 45) shows a young soldier saying goodbye to his mother before setting off for the annual troop review. The scene, painted on a *lekythos* (a type of vase placed on tombs), was probably commissioned by a woman to remind her of one of the happiest moments of her life. (There were few finer moments for a mother than when her son set off to become a soldier among soldiers and a citizen among citizens.) The vase dates from about 440 BC, during the high period of Athenian civilisation. Elegance of form, nobility and intimacy are fused in this scene, so elevated in tone and yet so unpretentiously human.

35. Inside of a cup. 490-480 BC. Martin von Wagner Museum, Würzburg.

36. Cup. 490-480 BC. Martin von Wagner Museum,
Würzburg.

35.   Inside of a cup. 490-480 BC. Martin von Wagner Museum, Würzburg. This comes from Vulci and is signed by Brygos as potter. The painter's name is unknown, and he is therefore known as the 'Brygos painter'. The subject is a unique variation on a theme—a courtesan helping a drunken youth who is being sick.

36.   Cup. 490-480 BC. Martin von Wagner Museum, Würzburg. This is the outside of the previous cup. It shows a procession of revellers and courtesans. The old man who is singing is declaring his desire for a young man. The young man does not seem interested, but the incident excites the jealousy of the old man at the end.

37.   Cup, c. 465 BC. Museum Antiker Kleinkunst, Munich. The drawing, fully emancipated from Archaic stiffness, has attained complete technical mastery. The painter, known as the 'Penthesilea painter' after this cup, was evidently impressed by the grandeur of this scene, which he had probably seen in the sculptures of the Theseum at Athens, and has enlarged the picture area to the maximum in order to paint figures of heroic proportions.

37. Cup, *c.* 465 BC. Museum Antiker Kleinkunst, Munich.

The ability of vase painters to produce humble works of ordinary human feeling is remarkable in view of the pressures on artists to produce grandiose works—the pressures of sculpture, painting, oratory, empire . . . Look at the tenderness with which the girl in plate 47 is drawn, standing on the tips of her toes to pick an apple from a tree; adolescence has rarely found such tender and lyrical expression. Equally impressive is the delicacy with which Sleep and the god of Death are portrayed laying a youth who fell fighting for his country on a sepulchral monument (plate 49); and the charm of the clouds dancing in the sky (plate 52). In plate 54 Eros (Love) and Anteros (Chastity) fight in the presence of Aphrodite and Artemis on a *pyxis* designed for a bride; in plate 53 a bride is preparing herself for her first night in the nuptial bed. In no branch of the visual arts have these painters been surpassed in portrayal of states of mind; the figures they paint are real people, not the cold abstractions of neo-classical imitation.

This art could also express regret for a loved one snatched away by death. This is done with great dignity, as in the case of the dead woman who is seated on the steps of her tomb immersed in the record of her past (plate 48). In this wonderful period nobility and simplicity go hand in hand with grace and lightness, especially in smaller works, which were immune from the temptations of pompousness and overstatement. Noble simplicity is combined with graceful femininity in the figure of a woman on a perfume vase, reproduced in plate 50, and the elegant and refined profile of the vase provides a harmonious and fitting frame.

Soon, however, elegance became affectation and simplicity an excuse for lack of imagination and lazy execution. And, paradoxically, advances in painting techniques led to the decline of vase painting. The famous paintings of the 5th century owe their greatness to that psychological penetration which no written source mentions, but to which these vases bear eloquent testimony. Their testimony in this respect is much more valuable than any evidence they provide about advances in rendering perspective. Technical progress is valuable, of course; but only in so far as it is subordinate to artistic vision: perspective techniques become useful and meaningful only when one wants to render an object at a distance. On the surface of a vase, however, this problem did not arise: nothing is less decorative than a face in three-quarter view, and the Greeks never painted land-scapes on their vases. (In the 7th century an attempt was made to do this, but the result can scarcely be termed successful.)

For this reason what we now think of as 'painting' became a 'major' art; vase painting sank to the status of a 'minor' art. The gulf between the two, which began about 470 BC, became increasingly deep. Towards 420 BC the decline of vase painting was rapid and perceptible, and after that date there are very few vases that can give complete aesthetic satisfaction. The development of tonality in painting was a contributory factor. The Greeks had already learnt the use of other colours than the white and red found on vases; Polygnotus certainly employed blue, yellow and green. But drawing remained the main skill involved; Greek paintings were really only coloured drawings until the time of Zeuxis. To judge from written sources, it was he who first created real paintings, substituting for the lines of drawing gradations of individual colours, and light and shade. It was a revolutionary step—so much so that ancient art historians deny the name of paint-

38. *Pelike.* 460-450 BC. Museo Provinciale Sigismondo Castromediano, Lecce.

38. *Pelike.* 460-450 BC. Museo Provinciale Sigismondo Castromediano, Lecce. From ancient Rudiae (modern Rugge). Polynices is offering Eriphyle the necklace of Harmonia. The details of the scene are executed with characteristic elegance; notice the simple robes, the hair and the stork.

39. Cup, *c.* 470 BC. British Museum, London. From Camiros, on the island of Rhodes. It is attributed to the Pistoxenos painter (Pistoxenos was the potter of a famous vase painted by this painter); some authorities identify him with the Penthesilea painter. The graceful and dignified Aphrodite riding a goose is perhaps the most noble portrayal of this figure.

40. Detail of a *crater, c.* 450 BC. Musée d'Art et d'Histoire, Geneva. The decoration is divided into two zones. At the top is the battle with the Amazons; below, a man in pursuit of four women. The two scenes are by different hands.

41. *Crater, c.* 450 BC. Musée d'Art et d'Histoire, Geneva. The vase is the only example of this style. It was inspired by Pauson, and the buyers did not like it.

42. Detail of a cup, *c.* 465 BC. Museum Antiker Kleinkunst, Munich. A detail of the outside edge of a cup by the Penthesilea painter. Both the outside and the inside of this cup have been attributed to the same painter, called by some the 'Penthesilea painter' and by others the 'horse painter'. But they are different in style and spirit and can scarcely be by the same hand.

39. Cup, *c.* 470 BC. British Museum, London.

40. Detail of a *crater, c.* 450 BC. Musée d'Art et d'Histoire, Geneva.

41. *Crater. c.* 450 BC. Musée d'Art et d'Histoire, Geneva.

42. Detail of a cup, *c.* 465 BC. Museum Antiker Kleinkunst, Munich.

ing to all that went before. It is reasonable to conclude that a promising young artist would no longer elect to become a vase painter; to him and his contemporaries the art must have seemed rudimentary, technically limited and lacking in scope for development; it was clear that the surface for a vase was not the place to experiment with the freedom possible in wall painting. Thus vase painting was destined to fall into the hands of people devoid of taste or sense of design.

The end of coloured drawing, however, came only slowly. The written sources refer to Parrhasius as a great artist—a consummate line artist who could capture the effects of light, shade and volume simply by using lines of varying thickness. But it was a foregone conclusion that, in the hands of less able craftsmen, such a polished technique would degenerate into affectation and mannerism. The most typical representative of this trend was Meidias. Plate 55 shows (above) Castor carrying off one of the daughters of Leucippus to his chariot, and (below) Hercules in the garden of the Hesperides. The poses are so mannered that it is difficult to believe that the painter was in earnest—though there can be no doubt that he was. He has sacrificed everything to a tasteless display of technical virtuosity, which is undoubtedly carried to its limit in his use of lines to indicate transparent garments, complicated folds and twisted hair.

Fortunately not all painters made the same mistake. The vase in plate 56 was painted at about the same time as Meidias' work. It shows Pelops arriving at the finishing post ahead of his rival, Oenomaos. The garments are thin and transparent with many folds, and Pelops' face is in the three-quarter view. The impression of speed is given by the fluttering cloak, the windswept hair and the horses' tails streaming in the wind; the hero is leaning backwards to control the horses. Pelops and his wife are staring keenly into the distance. Nothing is known about Parrhasius, but a painting like this perhaps gives us an idea of his greatness; it must be presumed that the anonymous painter of this vase was directly or indirectly influenced by his famous contemporary.

The two vases just discussed appear to date from the last phase of the Peloponnesian war. There is no stronger testimony to the Athenian spirit than the fact that, in spite of twenty years of war, simple

43. Detail of a *stamnos*. 500-490 BC. Museum Antiker Kleinkunst, Munich.

43.   Detail of a *stamnos*. 500-490 BC. Museum Antiker Klein-kunst, Munich. A *stamnos* is like an *amphora* but has a shorter neck. This one comes from Vulci. It is attributed to the Berlin painter, so called after a famous vase by him in the Berlin Museum. The scene is a contest between two heroes, held in the presence of Athena.

44.   *Lekythos*. 450-400 BC. Ashmolean Museum, Oxford. A *lekythos* is an oil-flask for use in burial rites. This is a white-ground example from Laurion in Attica. The decoration, prob-ably the work of the Achilles painter, consists of a woman hold-ing two vases containing oil for anointing the tomb.

45.   *Lekythos, c*. 440 BC. National Archaeological Museum, Athens. Observe the quiet and unaffected nobility of the woman's pose and the respectful and dignified young man. The perspective of the shield is correctly rendered in a three-quarter view. The objects above the woman are supposed to be hanging from a wall, and indicate that the figures are in an enclosed space.

46.   Calyx *crater*. 440-430 BC. Museo Gregoriano Etrusco, Vatican City. From Vulci. It is attributed to the Kleio painter. Note the free use of colour: this is the era of coloured drawing. Hercules is entrusting the young Dionysus to the care of the nymphs of Mount Nysa.

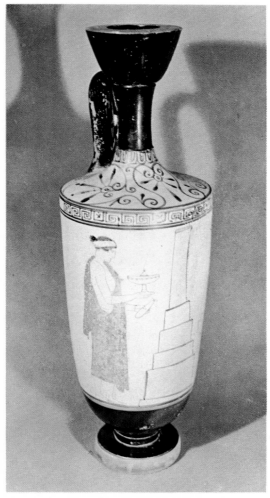

44. *Lekythos.* 450-400 BC. Ashmolean Museum, Oxford.

45. *Lekythos, c.* 440 BC. National Archaeological
Museum, Athens.

46. Calyx *crater*. 440-430 BC. Museo Gregoriano Etrusco,
Vatican City.

craftsmen could still be inspired by contemporary masterpieces to produce works such as these. But civil war and foreign occupation gave the quietus to the already flagging tradition of vase painting.

Attic vases of the first thirty years of the 4th century bear witness to the collapse of the Athenian Empire. They are almost without exception dull and monotonous, reflecting the disconsolate mood of their creators. The figures are either erect and stiff as dummies or, if they are in a group, strung together aimlessly and inorganically.

One of the very few exceptions to the general mediocrity is the *crater* of Pronomos (plate 57). It is so called because a famous Theban flautist, mentioned by Aristophanes in the *Ecclesiazusae,* which was produced in 390 BC, is represented on it (his name is written alongside). If it is really he that is represented, the vase can be dated to about the same period as the play. In contrast with vases of the previous period, colour has become much more important. Not that there is a great use of colours; but the number of figures with richly embroidered garments indicates a change in taste away from pure line. This preference is also visible in the rich decoration of the neck and handles. The treatment is very different from the simplicity of fifty years earlier, striving for effects similar to the monumentality of the great Dipylon vases. Perhaps this is no coincidence: when interest in drawing and ability to execute it declines, it is natural that there should be more interest in the profile of the vessel.

The subject of the Pronomos vase is a most interesting document of theatrical life at the time of Aristophanes. The three principal characters, Hercules, the king and an old Silenus (recognisable by the white furs stitched on to his garments and the mask with white hair and beard), are dressed for the parts but hold their respective masks in their hands. The Sileni, too, have their costumes on, and the poet, lyre-player and flautist are there. Also present are Dionysus and Ariadne, in whose honour the festival is being given. A performance is not in fact taking place; the actors are present just to provide a theatrical atmosphere.

In view of Athens' defeat in the Peloponnesian Wars and the decline in quality of Attic pottery, it is hardly surprising that Tarantum, the largest, richest and perhaps the most cultivated city of Magna

Graecia, began to produce pottery which often surpassed contemporary Attic products. Very often Tarantine products are monotonous and dull, but several works of great value were produced.

Tarantine pottery attracts our attention quite suddenly, with three masterpieces which date from the period between 420 and 410 BC. The subject of one of them (plate 60) is infrequently met with: Ulysses and Diomede about to capture Dolon, who is spying on the Greek camp. The most admirable feature is the way the characters of the three subjects are indicated. Up to now, in painting as in sculpture (to judge from such evidence as we have), feelings had been expressed, but never character. The sculptor Cresilas, a contemporary of Pheidias, for example, is praised for having made noble people even nobler. The portrait proper—the faithful reproduction of the particular characteristics of an individual—began in sculpture only towards 330 BC. It was anticipated around 379 BC by a type of portrait which was half-way between the generalised portrait of the 5th century and the realistic portrait of Hellenistic times—that is to say, one which attempted to capture the character and the spirit of the person, depicting

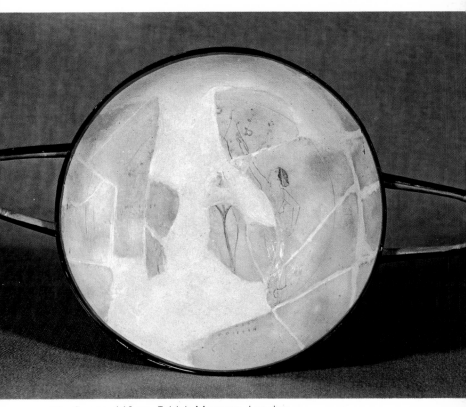

47. Cup, *c.* 440 BC. British Museum, London.

48. *Lekythos.* 430-420 BC. Museum Antiker
Kleinkunst, Munich.

49. *Lekythos, c.* 430 BC. British Museum, London.

47.   Cup, *c*. 440 BC. British Museum, London. This white-ground cup was found at Athens and is signed by Sotades as potter; the unknown painter is therefore called 'the Sotades painter'. The ancients always preferred to portray specific events, so the young girl should perhaps be interpreted as a Hesperide; whatever the intention, the figure is one of great charm.

48.   *Lekythos*. 430-420 BC. Museum Antiker Kleinkunst, Munich. White-ground *lekythos,* from Oropus. The woman, sitting in mourning by the tomb, is drawn in glaze; the ground on which she sits is painted.

49.   *Lekythos, c.* 430 BC. British Museum, London. From Ambelokipi, Attica. This vase was certainly painted with one of the victims of the Peloponnesian war in mind. Comparison with a Spartan product (plate 13) sums up the essential differences in outlook between the Athenians and the Spartans. The Spartans are braced for the glory of battle; the Athenians do not forget their humanity even when the war is at its grimmest

50.   Small *amphora* for perfume. 420-410 BC. Ashmolean Museum, Oxford. This vase is attributed to the Eretria painter. Note the folds of the drapery, which stream down like a cascade. They give the figure an extraordinary vitality.

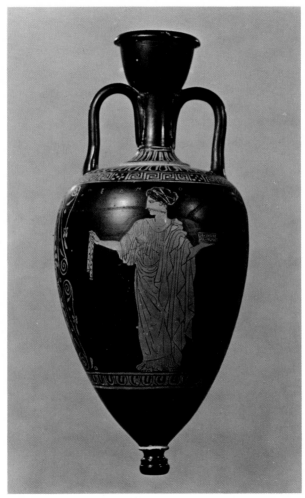

50. Small *amphora* for pertume. 420-410 BC.
Ashmolean Museum, Oxford.

only as much of his actual appearance as was necessary to express his character. No painted portrait before 350 BC has survived, but this vase, with its fine treatment of Dolon's cowardice, the impetuous but uncouth courage of Diomede and the prudent steadiness of Ulysses, suggests that character painting was not far away.

It is difficult to know whether the credit belongs to the vase painter or some other artist; and, for that matter, whether this new trend occurred in the mother country as well as Tarantum. After all, there was an ancient painting tradition in Greece which was still very much alive. Zeuxis, who was a very great master, is known to have worked for a long time in Magna Graecia. It is likely—though no written source says he painted portraits—that he exercised a profound influence in Tarantum, where the tradition of idealism was less strong than in Athens.

Another masterpiece of vase painting from Tarantum is on a magnificent volute *crater* (plate 59). It represents a religious ceremony held in the presence of Dionysus; its precise significance is not known. The god is sitting with his symbolic *thyrsus* and *kantharos* (the vessel with tall vertical handles which he holds in his left hand), in perfect serenity. He is watching the dance which a Maenad (recognisable from her *thyrsus*) performs to the music of the double flute. She does not move her feet, which are kept close together, but instead moves her body and head in a circle. (The Dervishes practise a similar dance today, at the end of which they fall insensible into a trance.) Behind her brother Dionysus stands Artemis with a water vessel in her left hand for ceremonial sprinkling, and shaking two torches to purify the atmosphere. On the extreme right a satyr leans against a column, watching the whole scene with detachment.

Everything about this work is remarkable, its total effect as much as its details. There is no discordant note. The twist of the dancer's head is part of the ritual, not a mannered pose. The whole ritual and artistic conception is different from that current in Greece. The robes of Artemis, for example, are very different from the simple Greek panther skin worn across the *chiton*. She wears a properly cut and shaped skin over a fine long-sleeved garment. The *thyrsus* which Dionysus holds, unlike the normal *thyrsus*, ends in a crown of five poppies. Finally there are the fine earrings of the flute-girl and the swirling dress of the dancing-girl, furrowed with folds reminiscent of ripples on water.

The previous two vases are part of a group called 'Proto-Italiot', which lasted until about 370 BC. The other products of this group are not of outstanding quality. From 370 to 330 BC Attic and Tarantine pottery developed along similar lines. In both there are a few works of excellent quality and many mediocre ones. Attic pottery of this period has been given the name of 'Kersch', from a place in the Crimea where numerous examples were found. For the same reason much Tarantine ware has been called 'Gnathia' ware, from a place in Apulia. The two types have several features in common but are quite different in many respects. They reached their peak in about the middle of the 4th century, although they continued to be produced until the beginning of the next century. (Significantly enough there was a limited revival of Athenian political power in the middle of the 4th century.)

I have chosen one example of Attic pottery of this period. It is a fine piece and very characteristic: 'the *oenochoe* of the procession' (plate 61). The artist has

51. Volute *crater, c.* 450 BC. Museo Nazionale Archeologico, Naples.

51. Volute *crater, c.* 450 BC. Museo Nazionale Archeologico, Naples. This vase, like others carrying the same subject, is inspired by the great Athenian masters who used the Battle with the Amazons as a subject for their wall paintings. But a series of fine figures does not necessarily produce a satisfactory overall effect.

52. Vase in the shape of a knuckle-bone, *c.* 450-400 BC. British Museum, London. From Aegina. Probably designed as a container for the game of knuckle-bones. The female figures are perhaps personifications of the winds or (more probably) the clouds. It is a fine example of Greek fantasy, beautiful and useful at the same time.

53. *Pyxis* (box). 440-430 BC. Martin von Wagner Museum, Würzburg. From Attica. A betrothed girl is combing her hair in preparation for her wedding. A cupid is bringing her a philtre which will make her irresistible.

54. *Pyxis.* 440-430 BC. Martin von Wagner Museum, Würzburg. The other side of the previous example. The two spirits in conflict are Eros and Anteros or Amor and Pudor. It is not by the Sotades painter, but by one of his pupils.

55. *Hydria.* 410 BC. British Museum, London. This vase almost certainly comes from Southern Italy. It is signed by Meidias as potter. All his pictures are mannered; in this case there is a great contrast between the effete poses and the violent action.

52. Vase in the shape of a knuckle-bone. 450-400 BC.
British Museum, London.

53. *Pyxis.* 440-430 BC. Martin von Wagner Museum, Würzburg.

54. *Pyxis.* 440-430 BC. Martin von Wagner Museum,
Würzburg.

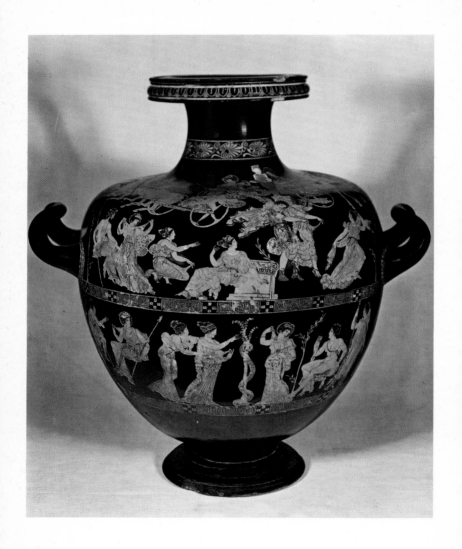

reduced the border to the minimum in order not to spoil the effect of the picture. There is just a fine band along the bottom which acts as a base for the figures, and an ivy chain around the neck. In the centre, a young woman has undone the knot which ties her *chiton* over her left shoulder, leaving the shoulder bare; she is holding the end of the knot in her mouth. In a moment she will appear quite naked before Dionysus, who is looking at her with admiring eyes. To the left is Eros, who accompanies the woman, removing his shoe. It is his task to keep the flames of love alive as long as necessary. The object between Eros and the woman is a ritual basket which indicates that the scene takes place in a temple. (It is, of course, the temple of Dionysus, his abode when he came down to earth to meet his worshippers; this was one of the functions of every temple.)

The form of a woman's body can be seen under her thin garments. This is typical of the period we are dealing with. (About 350 BC. At about this time Praxiteles had just sculpted his Venus for a sanctuary in Cos. Her body was covered—but revealed—by the transparent garments produced by the island.) Next to the woman is written the word 'procession',

55. *Hydria*. 410 BC. British Museum, London.

whence the name of the vase. It refers to the procession of worshippers who accompanied the wife of the King Archon to the temple of Dionysus, where she spent the night. This was a very ancient rite which reflected beliefs a thousand years older: to appease the god and persuade him to provide a favourable harvest, the king placed his wife at his disposal for one night. In the 4th century, however, the wife of the King Archon was generally a respectable elderly lady, more often than not a grandmother, whose charms were scarcely such as to attract a god. To write 'wife of the King Archon' next to a young woman in the prime of youth, offering herself to a god who was looking at her with eager desire in his eyes, would have been tantamount to a caricature. The painter therefore preferred to indicate her by the word 'procession', whose meaning would be clear enough to any Athenian.

The painting is very delicate and is inspired by tonal painting as developed by Zeuxis and practised by the great masters of the 4th century, and by the recent interest shown by artists in the female nude. It was not until about this time that artists realised the beauty of the female body, or thought of using it as a subject. This is one of the few Attic vases which displays the influence of the great pictorial revolution brought about by Zeuxis and his followers. Particularly striking is the use of white to distinguish the female body from the male.

This new preference for the female nude can be seen on another *pelike* of about the same period. It shows Peleus ravishing Thetis (plate 58). Thetis is nude (she was bathing at the sea shore), as is the magnificent flying Nereid on the shoulder of the vase. The drapery of the clothes worn by Peleus' helpers can compete in grace and elegance with the best works of the previous century.

In Southern Italy, perhaps through the influence of Zeuxis, who worked in Locris, colour became more important in the vase painting of the 4th century. Despite some incorrectness in the drawing, the big *crater* from Ruro (plate 62) remains a fine example of the work of the best craftsmen of Tarantum. Over the centuries, from the Geometric period onwards, the shape of the *crater* was slowly transformed; but the proportions, although they changed, always remained harmonious and true to the Greek canon. Even if the volutes set over the handles seem at first sight to be an excessive and heavy adjunct, closer scrutiny reveals that their removal would unbalance the piece. On the cover of the mixing bowl a Muse sits playing her lyre in a space bordered by an ivy bough; her hair and *chiton* are painted yellow and her mantle violet. This is painting proper, not coloured drawing. On the body of the vase is a painting of Orestes at Delphi, inside the temple. The hero grips the great sacred stone, the *omphalos,* with both hands. It is covered with a net and pieces of wool. The god prophesied from beside it. The god simply holds up his hand to drive away the Fury who is swooping down from the left. The god is so indignant that the Fury should commit the profanity of entering his temple that the priestess flees in terror. On the right, Artemis, who has just returned from the hunt and is accompanied by her hounds, is calmly watching. The votive gifts and sacred garments complete the scene.

Certainly there are imperfections; the gestures, for example, are somewhat exaggerated. But there are many beauties too, such as the rich use of white and the profuse details with which clothing and hair are rendered. Even the fluting on the Ionic columns is

56. *Amphora* with twisted handles. 420-410 BC.
Museo Archeologico, Arezzo.

57. Volute *crater, c.* 410 BC. Museo Nazionale Archeologico,
Naples.

58. *Pelike, c.* 350 BC. British Museum, London.

56.   *Amphora* with twisted handles. 420-410 BC. Museo Archeologico, Arezzo. The ardour of the horses, the energy of Pelops, the astonishment of Hippodamia, even the olive trees at the side of the road, are integral to the scene, and the result is balanced and harmonious.

57.   Volute *crater, c.* 410 BC. Museo Nazionale Archeologico, Naples. This is called the 'Pronomos vase' because on it is represented the flautist of that name mentioned by Aristophanes in his play the *Ecclesiazusae,* performed in 392 BC. The flautist was already famous in 420 BC.

58.   *Pelike, c.* 350 BC. British Museum, London. From Camiros on the island of Rhodes. It is of the school of the Marsyas painter. Note the traces of blue, green and gold; originally there were more colours.

59.   Volute *crater, c.* 410 BC. Museo Nazionale Archeologico, Taranto. From Ceglie in Apulia. The painter is called the Carneia painter from a scene by another hand on the other side, of the festival held in honour of Apollo Carneios. It is normally assigned to the end of the 5th century, though I would date it about 380 BC.

60.   Calyx *crater.* 410-400 BC. British Museum, London. It is generally thought that the painter, the Bowsprit painter, did not want to give a straightforward account of the Homeric story of the ambush of Dolon by Ulysses and Diomede, but instead turned it into a full-blooded, hilarious pantomime.

59. Volute *crater, c.* 410 BC. Museo Nazionale Archeologico. Taranto.

indicated with dilute glaze: assuming it to be yellow, one imagines that the shafts were gilded.

Few Tarantine vases maintain this high quality. There are two parallel styles: the type with coloured paintings on a uniformly black ground; and the red-figure style. The first is the 'Gnathian' style, of which the earliest examples, dating from 360—330 BC are rarely repetitive, and all have some interesting and admirable features. There are few surviving examples, and of these few there is only space for two in this book.

The first (plate 63) is only a fragment, but fortunately the essential part is preserved. It shows an actor who has taken off his mask to receive the applause of the audience. He is a king in a tragedy, probably Oedipus. The vase dates from about 350 BC, the period when true portraiture began. No anatomical details are indicated, but typical characteristics are shown. The actor, balding and unshaven, has a weary expression on his face—whether because he is tired of bowing to a public that believes itself so much his superior, or because he is immersed in the fantasy world of the play, it is impossible to know. His face contrasts strongly with the noble face

60. Calyx *crater.* 410-400 BC. British Museum, London.

of the king on the tragic mask. Is this contrast deliberate? Or did the artist simply wish to depict a theatrical prop? If the latter, he painted the mask merely because it was part of an actor's equipment— like the sword, the purple cloak and so on. The first hypothesis is the more attractive, but the second is probably correct.

The fragment is also interesting for a technical detail. The point of the actor's nose and of the nose of his mask, and the cheek-bone of the mask are highlighted in white paint. The painter has attempted to show reflections of the light on points where it strikes directly. The Greeks always aspired to paint realistically, and progressed slowly and steadily for centuries. Now, long after they had discovered how to render light and shade, they discovered how to render reflections. Curiously enough, they first used it only on the male body; this is well attested by written evidence and figurative art.

In connection with this point it is worth studying one of the finest examples of Tarantine ware, the 'Aurora' *crater* (plate 64), which comes from Latium and is kept in the Villa Giulia Museum at Rome. Eos is rising from the sea in a chariot, accompanied by the young Kephalos, whom she has seduced; in front of them is Phosphorus, the morning star. The lovers are looking at each other with intense affection. The cranes flying through the air and the dolphins darting through the waves complete the atmosphere of bright and joyful dawn. The profile of the *crater*, with its high volutes above the rim and the stylised antelopes' heads at the springing of the handles, was later to become common in Tarantine pottery. The decoration is opulent, but avoids the excesses of bad taste. The series of palmettes and lotus leaves above the animal frieze is at once rich and delicate; it harmonises perfectly with the painting without overwhelming it.

After 330 BC there was little vase painting of artistic merit in Attica. Both economically and socially there was too big a gap between the great artists and the craftsmen who, in order to survive, had to produce quantity rather than quality. But fine works were occasionally produced. Some idea of developments in vase painting can be gleaned from written sources, but it was a period of some obscurity, and few names are recorded. The calyx *crater* from Attica (plate 65), which dates from about 310 BC, is clearly very late because of its extremely elongated profile. The three painted figures are still perfectly adapted to the proportions of the vase. The muscular figure of Hercules is successful, but the two goddesses are very gangling creatures. They conform to the canon of Lysippus, whose statues were seven times the height of the head, instead of the six times of Polycleitus. Two centuries were to pass before such slender female figures are found again.

This vase is one of the best products of Attic pottery of the last three decades of the 4th century. The others are more often than not rushed off carelessly and without pride. Very few examples are found outside Attica because nobody wanted them any more: a completely new form of pottery had been invented by an Athenian potter called Thericles. This was pottery with reliefs, completely glazed. Thericles was a man of artistic taste, with a flair for business. At the beginning of the Peloponnesian war he became convinced that the golden age of pot painting was over, and he therefore experimented with this new art form. He realised that a cheap substitute for metal vases—with colour to aid the illusion of expense—would be in great demand.

61. Attic *oenochoe, c.* 350 BC. Metropolitan Museum of Art, New York.

62. Volute *crater* with cover. 360 BC. Museo Nazionale
Archeologico, Naples.

63. Fragment of a bell *crater*. 350-340 BC. Martin von
Wagner Museum, Würzburg.

61.   Attic *oenochoe, c.* 350 BC. Metropolitan Museum of Art, New York. Fletcher Fund, 1925. The wife of the King Archon of Athens is taking off her clothes in the presence of Dionysus. Apart from the mythological content it serves to illustrate Attic marriage custom, which required that the bride undressed alone.

62.   Volute *crater*. 360 BC. Museo Nazionale Archeologico, Naples. The cover is painted in the Gnathian style, while the body is done in the standard red-figure technique. It is one of the oldest examples of the Gnathian style, but it is only used on a secondary part of the vessel.

63   Fragment of a bell *crater*. 350-340 BC. Martin von Wagner Museum, Würzburg. From Taranto. Apart from its artistic merit, this vase is interesting because it testifies to the enthusiasm for the theatre at Tarantum. It shows an actor removing his mask and taking a bow.

64.   Volute *crater, c.* 360 BC. Museo di Villa Giulia, Rome. Called the 'Aurora *crater'* because the principal figures in the scene are Eos (Aurora, i.e. dawn) and Kephalos being carried across a starry sky in a chariot. The sea below is full of monsters.

65.   Calyx *crater*. 310 BC. National Archeological Museum, Athens. Hercules is standing between Athena and a wingless Victory who is garlanding his head with a wreath. This is one of the standard ways of expressing the apotheosis of heroes.

64. Volute *crater, c.* 360 BC. Museo di Villa Giulia, Rome.

65. Calyx *crater.* 310 BC. National Archaeological Museum,
Athens.

However, commercial success was still unthinkable unless such vases possessed artistic merit. In fact Thericles' vases are more than once praised in 4th-century comedies, which testifies to the favour they enjoyed and the esteem in which they were held. Naturally he very soon mass-produced them and, by reducing to a minimum the painted or incised decoration or omitting it completely, was able to produce a vase in which little brush work was involved. They are attractive pieces, especially the smaller vases.

At Tarantum both Gnathian and red-figure pottery continued to flourish in the last three decades of the 4th century. The first was primarily designed for banquets, including of course funeral banquets; the second was almost exclusively for funerary use, which explains the enormous number which have been preserved. Gnathian pottery declined rapidly, as so frequently happens when demand becomes heavy; and Tarantine red-figure pottery was repetitive—which is not surprising considering that its patrons purchased it only for funerary use.

Although funerary themes constituted the subject of the vast majority of Tarantine red-figure vases, several large *craters* were produced with paintings of popular myths inspired by contemporary epics, or of theatrical scenes. Details of two of these are illustrated. The size of these *craters* was exceptional, and makes it difficult to believe that they ever served a practical purpose. They were used primarily as ornaments for the house, and later for the tomb. (The region had no marble for gravestones and was probably by now poor in timber.)

The subject of the 'Vase of Patroclus' (plate 66) is less interesting to us than it was to contemporaries. We are more interested in a dull historical fact than in a heroic mythical episode. But in classical antiquity the heroic myth was not clearly distinguished from— and was certainly as valid as—history. On this vase there are three zones, each one corresponding to a different episode in the story of Patroclus. On the top, the gods are discussing the consequences of the death of Patroclus; in the middle, Achilles is slaughtering a Trojan prisoner in front of the pyre on which Patroclus' body lies; at the bottom, Achilles is returning on his chariot after dragging the body of Hector round the walls of Troy.

Technically speaking, the most interesting features

66. Detail of an Apulian *crater*. 340 BC. Museo Nazionale Archeologico, Naples.

66. Detail of an Apulian *crater*. 340 BC. Museo Nazionale Archeologico, Naples. This *crater* is also called the 'Patroclus vase' from the subject in the central zone. The incidents in the three zones are not parts of a single scene; each is complete in itself.

67. Detail of a *crater*. 340 BC. Museo Nazionale Archeologico, Naples. Found in a tomb at Canosa. A satrap (Persian provincial governor) is talking to the King of Persia and is standing on a golden plinth, exactly as described by the historian Herodotus.

68. Fragment of a calyx *crater*. 340-330 BC. Museo di Villa Giulia, Rome. From Buccino (Salerno). It is signed by Assteas as painter. The expressions on the faces of the three figures are exaggerated in the manner of caricatures to convey their feelings: anger in Cassandra, terror in Ajax and alarm in the priestess.

69. Large plate. 284 BC. Museo di Villa Giulia, Rome. From Capena in Latium. This is generally considered to be a work of the settlers at Tarantum and is therefore often dated after 276 BC. the year of the capture and sack of Tarantum. In my view, however, it was painted in Tarantum in 284 BC.

67. Detail of a *crater*. 340 BC. Museo Nazionale Archeologico, Naples.

are the free use of shading and shadows, and the reflections thrown back by the glint of the armour. Considering how poor other vases of the period were, these rare details of technique are of value because they give some idea how the great artists of the 4th century handled colour.

The scene in the middle of the '*crater* of the Persians' (plate 67) is easy to identify: the name of each character is written next to the figure. Darius sits

68. Fragment of a calyx *crater*. 340-330 BC. Museo di Villa Giulia, Rome.

69. Large plate. 284 BC. Museo di Villa Giulia, Rome.

on his throne, guarded by a bodyguard who stands behind him. He and a group of Persian noblemen are listening to an old man who is addressing them. He is probably a satrap from the coast of the Aegean Sea who knows the Greeks at first hand and is warning the king that they are formidable opponents. Greek bias appears in the jibe on the lowest zone. The king's treasurer points out on the account sheet how much money the citizens owe . . . but they hold out empty hands. The remaining scenes of the vase—a battle with the Amazons, Bellerophon killing the Chimaera, and a lethargic group of satyrs and Maenads—are very inferior to the main scene, and are probably not by the same master. His skill is displayed in the faces of Darius, the counsellors and the treasurer; the faces of the gods are rather inexpressive. The faces of the mortals are not, however, true portraits: Darius I had been dead for a considerable time, and during his lifetime no artist would have thought of portraying him realistically.

Poseidonia, later called Paestum, was a Greek city near Tarantum. The fragment in plate 68 is in the Paestan style, and is such as to make possible reconstruction of the subject and something of the spirit of the pottery. It is a parody of the mythological episode in which Ajax attacked Cassandra in the Sanctuary of Athena and tore her from the statue of the goddess. In all other versions of the scene the virgin vainly holds on to the statue; but here she not only successfully defends herself, but retaliates with such vigour that the unfortunate Ajax has to hang on to the statue himself; Cassandra is so angry that she has seized him by the crest of his helmet. Nothing remains of Cassandra's face except her left eye, but that is threatening enough to explain the unconcealed fear of the hero. The old priestess flees in fear, but the goddess is winking and seems to be enjoying herself, entertained by the change of fortune being enacted under her eyes.

Previous Tarantine painters had no intention of making caricatures (whatever our feelings about their efforts may be); here it was evidently the intention. It is not necessarily that Assteas was sceptical and derided religion and the heroic past, but simply that the comic theatre had diffused an irreverent spirit throughout the world of culture. (Aristophanes had gingerly initiated this trend at the beginning of the 4th century.) Once again the best

Italiot pottery, and Siciliot too, from what is known of other fragments, is inspired by the theatre.

The example of the final phase of Greek pottery (plate 69) with which this book ends is interesting for its subject-matter and valuable chronologically. It is a plate executed in the Gnathian technique, with colour on an entirely glazed ground. (Very little of the characteristic decoration of this type of pottery remains, and what does remain is of poor quality.) In the centre is a war elephant with a baby elephant which has twisted its trunk around its mother's tail for fear of losing her. The elephant's guide sits on its neck, and on its back is set a turret which contains four soldiers. The march-past which Pyrrhus organised shortly after his landing at Tarantum in 284 BC was clearly very much in the mind of the artist, which suggests that the plate was made shortly after the event. Later, the Tarantines would have had little chance to see the elephants which were mobilised against the Romans; and the disastrous end of the expedition was such as to make a Tarantine artist unlikely to recall the march-past willingly. The fall of the city dealt the final blow to an art form which had flourished in the Greek world for seven centuries.

LIST OF ILLUSTRATIONS

Page